The New Novello Choral Edition

LUDWIG VAN BEETHOVEN

Choral Symphony

(Last Movement)

for soprano, alto, tenor and bass soli, SATB and orchestra

German text by Johann Christoph Friedrich von Schiller
English version by Natalia Macfarren

Revised by Michael Pilkington

Order No: NOV 072490

NOVELLO PUBLISHING LIMITED

It is requested that on all concert notices and programmes acknowledgement is made to 'The New Novello Choral Edition'.
Es wird gebeten, auf sämtlichen Konzertankündigungen und Programmen 'The New Novello Choral Edition' als Quelle zu erwähnen.
Il est exigé que toutes les notices et programmes de concerts, comportent des remerciements à 'The New Novello Choral Edition'.

Cover illustration: first vocal entry in the last movement of Beethoven's *Choral Symphony* from Schott's 1826 edition.

Published in Great Britain by Novello Publishing Limited

Exclusive distributors
Hal Leonard 7777 West Bluemound Road, Milwaukee, WI 53213
Email: info@halleonard.com

Hal Leonard Europe Limited 42 Wigmore Street Maryleborne,London, WIU 2 RY
Email: info@halleonardeurope.com

Hal Leonard Australia Pty. Ltd. 4 Lentara Court Cheltenham, Victoria, 9132 Australia
Email: info@halleonard.com.au

PREFACE

This vocal score has been revised in the light of the first edition of the full sco
and the full score published by Breitkopf & Härtel as part of the Gesamt.
reduction by Berthold Tours has been modified in places to bring it more into line with the full score.

NOTES

Bar 331 [Page 12 (52)]: the tempo mark here has been the subject of some discussion. Jonathan Del Mar's invaluable critical commentary[1] provides a convincing argument for considering the dotted crotchet = 84 an error for dotted minim = 84.

Bar 758 [Page 40 (80)]: there is considerable disagreement between editors as to the correct notes in this bar[2]. All are agreed that the wind parts (the right hand in this vocal score) have C naturals from the start of the bar; however, in the sources, the viola has a C natural throughout the bar, while the Chorus Altos have a sharp on the first beat. Some editors have suggested giving the Chorus Altos a natural on the first beat, others, including Schenker[3], sharpen the first viola note, only moving to a natural on the second beat. This is the version printed here, to agree with the hire material provided by the publishers.

Bar 851 [Page 51 (91)]: Beethoven appears to have changed his mind over the tempo marking here, altering **Prestissimo** to **Presto**, though it is possible he changed it back to **Prestissimo** later[4].

Bar 920 [Page 57 (97)]: Del Mar[5] suggests semibreve = 88 as the metronome mark for this section, on the evidence of Beethoven's conversation books.

Michael Pilkington
Old Coulsdon, February 1999

1 Johnathan Del Mar, *Beethoven Symphony No. 9 in D Minor Critical Commentary* (Bärenreiter 1996), p.56
2 Ibid. p.65
3 Heinrich Schenker (trans. Jonathan Rothgeb), *Beethoven's 9th Symphony* (Newhaven and London, 1992), pp.301-2
4 Del Mar, op. cit., p.67
5 Ibid. p.69

NOTE

Apart from the page 1 of this vocal score, where an extra eight bars have been added, this revised edition of *The last movement of the Choral Symphony* follows the layout of the previous edition (catalogue number NOV070047) page for page, to allow this new edition to be used side-by-side with the edition it supersedes. The page numbering of this revised edition starts with page 1. The numbering system of the previous edition (which started with page 41) is retained in brackets in small type.

CHORAL SYMPHONY

(LAST MOVEMENT)

This vocal score begins at the beginning of the second Presto section (bar 208) of the Finale of Beethoven's Symphony No.9.

237
Allegro assai
BARITONE SOLO
Praise her, praise, oh praise to Joy, the
Freu - de, Freu - de, Freu - de, schö - ner
Chorus
BASS
Praise her, praise her,
Freu - de, Freu - de!,
Allegro assai
Wind
p dolce
Horn
Str. pizz.
pp Ob.
p
242
God de - scend - ed Daugh - ter of E - ly - si - um, Ray of mirth and rap - ture blend - ed,
Göt - ter - fun - ken, Toch - ter aus E - ly - si - um, wir be - tre - ten Feu - er - trun - ken
Cl.
pp
p
247
God - dess, to thy shrine we come. By thy ma - gic is u - ni - ted what stern Cus - tom
Himm - li - sche, dein Hei - lig - tum! Dei - ne Zau - ber bin - den wie - der, was die Mo - de
252
part - ed wide, All man - kind are bro - thers plight - ed where thy gen - tle wings a - bide.
streng ge - teilt; al - le Men - schen wer - den Brü - der, wo dein sanf - ter Flü - gel weilt.
cresc.
p

257
Chorus
SOPRANO
f ALTO
By thy ma - gic is u - ni - ted What stern_ Cus - tom part - ed wide, All___
Dei - ne Zau - ber bin - den_ wie - der, was die_ Mo - de streng ge - teilt; al -
f TENOR
By thy ma - gic is u - ni - ted What stern_ Cus - tom part - ed wide, All___
Dei - ne Zau - ber bin - den_ wie - der, was die_ Mo - de streng ge - teilt; al -
f BASS
By thy ma - gic is u - ni - ted What stern_ Cus - tom part - ed wide, All___
Dei - ne Zau - ber bin - den_ wie - der, was die_ Mo - de streng ge - teilt; al -
257
f Tutti
Str. arco
261
___ man - kind are bro - thers plight - ed Where thy gen - tle wings a-bide.
- le Men - schen wer - den Brü - der, wo dein sanf - ter Flü - gel weilt.
___ man - kind are bro - thers plight - ed Where thy gen - tle wings a-bide.
- le Men - schen wer - den Brü - der, wo dein sanf - ter Flü - gel weilt.
___ man - kind are bro - thers plight - ed Where thy gen - tle wings a-bide.
- le Men - schen wer - den Brü - der, wo dein sanf - ter Flü - gel weilt.
261
sempre f

265
ALTO SOLO
Ye to whom the
Wem der gros - se
TENOR SOLO
Ye to whom the
Wem der gros - se
BASS SOLO
Ye to whom the_
Wem der gros - se__
265
8
Horn
p dolce
Vc.
270
SOPRANO SOLO
Who a wife has won and trea - sur'd
wer ein hol - des Weib er - run - gen
boon is mea - sur'd Friend to be of faith - ful friend, Who a wife has won and trea - sur'd
Wurf ge - lun - gen, ei - nes Freun - des Freund zu sein, wer ein hol - des Weib er - run - gen
boon is mea - sur'd Friend to be__ of__ faith - ful friend,___ Who a wife has_ won_ and_ trea - sur'd_
Wurf ge - lun - gen, ei - nes Freun - des_ Freund zu sein,_____ wer ein hol - des_ Weib_ er - run - gen_
boon_ is__ mea - sur'd_ Friend to be of faith - ful friend,___ Who a wife has_ won_ and_ trea - sur'd_
Wurf_ ge - lun - gen,_ ei - nes Freun - des Freund zu sein,_____ wer ein hol - des_ Weib_ er - run - gen_
270
Fl.
Vc.

275
To our strain your voi - ces lend, Yea, if a - ny hold in_ keep - ing On - ly_ one heart
mis - che sei - nen Ju - bel ein! Ja, wer auch nur ei - ne_ See - le sein nennt_ auf dem
To our strain your voi - ces lend,_ Yea, if a - ny_ hold in keep - ing_ On - ly_ one heart
mis - che sei - nen Ju - bel ein!_ Ja, wer auch nur_ ei - ne See - le_ sein_ nennt_ auf dem
To our strain your_ voi - ces lend,_ Yea, if a - ny_ hold in_ keep - ing_ On - ly_ one heart
mis - che sei - nen_ Ju - bel ein!_ Ja, wer auch nur_ ei - ne_ See - le_ sein_ nennt_ auf dem
To our strain your voi - ces lend, Yea,_ if a - ny hold_ in_ keep - ing On - ly one heart
mis - che sei - nen Ju - bel ein! Ja,_ wer auch nur ei - ne_ See - le sein nennt auf dem
275
Fl.
280
cresc. sf dim.
all his own, Let_ him join us, or else weep - ing, Steal from out our
Er - den - rund! Und_ wer's nie ge - konnt, der steh - le wei - nend sich aus
all his own, Let_ him join us, or else weep - ing, Steal from out our
Er - den - rund! Und_ wer's nie ge - konnt, der steh - le wei - nend sich aus
all his own, Let_ him join us, or else weep - ing, Steal from out our
Er - den - rund! Und_ wer's nie ge - konnt, der steh - le wei - nend sich aus
all his own, Let_ him join us,_ or_ else_ weep - ing,_ Steal from out our
Er - den - rund! Und_ wer's nie ge - konnt,_ der_ steh - le_ wei - nend sich aus
280
cresc. dim. p

284

midst, un-known.
dei - sem Bund.

midst, un-known.
dei - sem Bund.

midst, un-known.
dei - sem Bund.

midst, un - known.
dei - sem Bund.

284

Chorus SOPRANO *f*

Yea, if a - ny hold in-keep - ing On - ly_ one heart all his own, Let_
*Ja, wer auch nur ei - ne_ See - le sein nennt_ auf dem Er - den-rund! Und_*

ALTO *f*

Yea, if a - ny hold in keep - ing_ On - ly one heart all his own, Let_
*Ja, wer auch nur ei - ne See - le_ sein nennt auf dem Er - den-rund! Und_*

TENOR *f*

Yea, if a - ny hold in_ keep - ing_ On - ly one heart all his own, Let_
*Ja, wer auch nur ei - ne_ See - le_ sein nennt auf dem Er - den-rund! Und_*

BASS *f*

Yea,_ if a - ny hold in keep - ing On - ly one heart all his own, Let_
*Ja,_ wer auch nur ei - ne See - le sein nennt auf dem Er - den-rund! Und_*

284

cresc. *f* Tutti

289

sf *dim.* *p*

_ him join us, or else weep - ing, Steal from out our midst, un-known.
_ wer's nie ge - konnt, der steh - le wei - nend sich aus dei - sem Bund.

sf *dim.* *p*

_ him join us, or else weep - ing, Steal from out our midst, un-known.
_ wer's nie ge - konnt, der steh - le wei - nend sich aus dei - sem Bund.

sf *dim.* *p*

_ him join us, or else weep - ing, Steal from out our midst, un-known.
_ wer's nie ge - konnt, der steh - le wei - nend sich aus dei - sem Bund.

sf *dim.* *p*

_ him join us,_ or_ else weep - ing,_ Steal from out our midst, un - known.
_ wer's nie ge - konnt,_ der_ steh - le_ wei - nend sich aus dei - sem Bund.

294
TENOR SOLO
Draughts of joy, from
Freu - de trin - ken
BASS SOLO
Draughts of joy, from
Freu - de trin - ken
294
sempre p
tr
Vc.
Horns
298
ALTO SOLO
Grace to just and
Al - - le Gu - ten,
cup o'er - flow - ing, Boun-teous Na - ture free - ly gives Grace to just and
al - le We - sen an den Brü - sten der Na - tur; Al - le Gu - ten,
cup o'er - flow - ing, Boun-teous Na - ture free - ly gives Grace to just and
al - le We - sen an den Brü - sten der Na - tur; Al - le Gu - ten,
298
Vla.
Vln.
Bsn.

302
SOPRANO SOLO
Wine she gave to
Küs - se gab sie
un - just shew - ing, Bless - ing ev - 'ry thing that lives. Wine she gave to
al - le Bö - sen fol - gen ih - rer Ro - sen - spur. Küs - se gab sie
un - just shew - ing, Bless - ing ev - 'ry thing that lives. Wine she gave to
al - le Bö - sen fol - gen ih - rer Ro - sen - spur. Küs - se gab sie
un - just shew - ing, Bless - ing ev - 'ry thing that lives. Wine she gave to
al - le Bö - sen fol - gen ih - rer Ro - sen - spur. Küs - se gab sie
302
tr
sempre p
306
us, and kiss - es, Loy - al friend on life's steep road, E'en
uns und Re - ben, ei - nen Freund, ge - prüft im Tod; Wol -
us, and kiss - es, Loy - al friend on life's steep road, E'en
uns und Re - ben, ei - nen Freund, ge - prüft im Tod; Wol -
us, and kiss - es, Loy - al friend on life's steep road, E'en
uns und Re - ben, ei - nen Freund, ge - prüft im Tod; Wol -
us, and kiss - es, Loy - al friend on life's steep road, E'en
uns und Re - ben, ei - nen Freund, ge - prüft im Tod; Wol -
306
tr

309
cresc.
the worm can feel life's bliss - es, And the Se - raph
lust ward dem Wurm ge - ge - ben, und der Che - rub
tr
312
dwells with God.
steht vor Gott.
Chorus
SOPRANO [f]
ALTO [f]
TENOR [f]
BASS [f]
Wine she gave to us, and kiss - es,
Küs - se gab sie uns und Re - ben,
Tutti
sempre f

315
Loy - al friend on life's steep road, E'en the worm can
ei - nen Freund, ge - prüft im Tod; Wol - - lust ward dem
sempre più f
318
feel life's bliss - es, And the Se - raph dwells with God,
Wurm ge - ge - ben, und der Che - rub steht vor Gott,
sf
ff

321

and the Se - raph dwells with God, dwells with
und der Che - rub steht vor Gott, steht vor

sf

and the Se - raph dwells with God, dwells with
und der Che - rub steht vor Gott, steht vor

and the Se - raph dwells with God, dwells with
und der Che - rub steht vor Gott, steht vor

and the Se - raph dwells with God, dwells with
und der Che - rub steht vor Gott, steht vor

321

ben marcato

326

ff *ff* *ff*

God, with God, with God.
Gott, vor Gott, vor Gott.

ff *ff* *ff*

God, with God, with God.
Gott, vor Gott, vor Gott.

ff *ff* *ff*

God, with God, with God.
Gott, vor Gott, vor Gott.

ff *ff* *ff*

God, with God, with God.
Gott, vor Gott, vor Gott.

326

ff *ff*

molto tenuto

* Probably ♩. = 84 intended, see Preface

375
TENOR SOLO
Glad, glad, glad, as his suns, the suns His
Froh, froh, wie sei - ne Son - nen, sei - ne
Wind
381
will sent ply - ing, as the suns His will sent ply - ing
Son - nen flie - gen, froh, wie sei - ne Son - nen flie - gen
poco cresc.
387
Through the vast a - byss of space, Bro - thers, run your
durch des Him - mels prächt' - gen Plan, lau - fet, Brü - der,
poco cresc.
393
joy - ous race, bro - thers, run your joy - ous race,
eu - re Bahn, lau - fet, Brü - der, eu - re Bahn,

399
He - ro - like to con - quest fly - ing, on, to con -
freu - dig, wie ein Held zum Sie - gen, wie ein Held
399
poco f
405
- quest fly - ing, Bro - thers, run your joy - ous race,
zum Sie - gen, lau - fet, Brü - der, eu - re Bahn,
405
411
Chorus
TENOR
411
div. [mf]
Bro - thers, run your joy - ous race, He - ro -
Lau - fet Brü - der, eu - re Bahn, freu - dig,
BASS
[mf]
Bro - thers, run your joy - ous race, He - ro -
Lau - fet Brü - der, eu - re Bahn, freu - dig,
411
più f
più f

416
on, to con - -
wie ein Held
- like to con - quest fly - ing, on, to con - -
wie ein Held zum Sie - gen, wie ein Held
- like to con - quest fly - ing, on, to con - -
wie ein Held zum Sie - gen, wie ein Held
più f

421
- quest fly - - - ing.
zum Sie - - - gen.
- quest fly - ing, Joy - ous,
zum Sie - gen, freu - dig,
- quest fly - ing, Joy - ous,
zum Sie - gen, freu - dig,
sf
ff

(N.B. Diese 6 Takte können nicht von Chor wohl aber von dem Solosänger ausgellassen werden)*

* These six bars may be omitted by the soloist but not by the chorus

459
sf
sf
sf
sf
465
sf
sf
sf
sf
sf
471
477
8
483
8
488
sf
sf

493
sf
499
505
511
517
ff
525
Horns
dim.
Ob.
p
Str.
più p
534
pp
sempre pp
cresc.

Chorus
543
f SOPRANO
Praise to Joy, the God descend - ed Daugh - ter of E -
Freu - de, schö - ner Göt - ter - fun - ken, Toch - ter aus E -
f ALTO
Praise to Joy, the God de - scend - ed Daugh - ter of E -
Freu - de, schö - ner Göt - ter - fun - ken, Toch - ter aus E -
f TENOR
Praise to Joy, the God de - scend - ed Daugh - ter of E -
Freu - de, schö - ner Göt - ter - fun - ken, Toch - ter aus E -
f BASS
Praise to Joy, the God de - scend - ed Daugh - ter of E -
Freu - de, schö - ner Göt - ter - fun - ken, Toch - ter aus E -
543
ff Tutti
549
sf
- ly - si - um, Ray of mirth and rap - ture blend - ed,
- ly - si - um, wir be - tre - ten feu - er - trun - ken,
549

555
God - dess, to thy shrine we come. By thy ma - gic
Himm - li - sche, dein Hei - lig - tum! Dei - ne Zau - ber
sf
561
is u - ni - ted What stern Cus - tom part - ed wide, All
bin - den wie - der, was die Mo - de streng ge - teilt; al -
ff

567
sf
— man - kind are bro - thers plight - ed Where thy gen - tle
- le Men - schen wer - den Brü - der, wo dein sanf - ter
sf
— man - kind are bro - thers plight - ed Where thy gen - tle
- le Men - schen wer - den Brü - der, wo dein sanf - ter
sf
— man - kind are___ bro - thers plight - ed Where thy gen - tle
- le Men - schen___ wer - den Brü - der, wo dein sanf - ter
sf
— man - kind are bro - thers plight - ed Where thy gen - tle
- le Men - schen wer - den Brü - der, wo dein sanf - ter
567
573
wings___ a - bide. By thy ma - gic is u -
Flü - gel weilt. Dei - ne Zau - ber bin - den___
wings___ a - bide. By thy ma - gic is u -
Flü - gel weilt. Dei - ne Zau - ber bin - den
wings___ a - bide. By thy ma - gic is u -
Flü - gel weilt. Dei - ne Zau - ber bin - den___
wings___ a - bide. By thy ma - gic is u -
Flü - gel weilt. Dei - ne Zau - ber bin - den
573

578
ff
-ni - ted What stern___ Cus - tom part - ed wide, All___
wie - der, was die___ Mo - de streng ge - teilt; al -
-ni - ted What stern___ Cus - tom part - ed wide, All___
wie - der, was die___ Mo - de streng ge - teilt; al -
-ni - ted What stern___ Cus - tom part - ed wide, All___
wie - der, was die___ Mo - de streng ge - teilt; al -
-ni - ted What stern Cus - tom part - ed wide, All___
wie - der, was die Mo - de streng ge - teilt; al -
583
sf
___ man - kind are bro - thers plight - ed Where thy gen - tle
- le Men - schen wer - den Brü - der, wo dein sanf - ter
___ man - kind are bro - thers plight - ed Where thy gen - tle
- le Men - schen wer - den Brü - der, wo dein sanf - ter
___ man - kind are___ bro - thers plight - ed Where thy gen - tle
- le Men - schen___ wer - den Brü - der, wo dein sanf - ter
___ man - kind are bro - thers plight - ed Where thy gen - tle
- le Men - schen wer - den Brü - der, wo dein sanf - ter

589
wings a - bide.
Flü - gel weilt.
wings a - bide.
Flü - gel weilt.
wings a - bide.
Flü - gel weilt.
wings a - bide.
Flü - gel weilt.
589
sf
sf
595 Andante maestoso (𝅗𝅥 = 72)
ff
ff
ff
O ye mil-lions, I em - brace ye! Here's a joy - ful kiss for all!
Seid um-schlun-gen, Mil - li - o - nen! Die - sen Kuss der gan - zen Welt!
ff
ff
ff
O ye mil-lions, I em - brace ye! Here's a joy - ful kiss for all!
Seid um - schlun-gen, Mil - li - o - nen! Die - sen Kuss der gan - zen Welt!
595 Andante maestoso (𝅗𝅥 = 72)
Trb., Vc., Cb.
ff
sf
sf
sf
sf
Str.
f

604
O ye mil - lions, I em - brace ye!
Seid um - schlun - gen, Mil - - li - o - nen!
O ye mil - lions, I em - brace ye! Here's
Seid um - schlun - gen, Mil - - li - o - nen! Die -
O ye mil - lions, I em - brace ye!
Seid um - schlun - gen, Mil - li - o - nen!
O ye mil - lions, I em - brace ye!
Seid um - schlun - gen, Mil - - li - o - nen!
604
Wind sustain
608
Here's a kiss, a kiss for all!
Die - - sen Kuss der gan - zen Welt!
a kiss, a kiss for all!
- - sen Kuss der gan - zen Welt!
Here's a joy - ful kiss for all!
Die - sen Kuss der gan - zen Welt!
Here's a joy - ful kiss for all!
Die - - sen Kuss der gan - zen Welt!
608

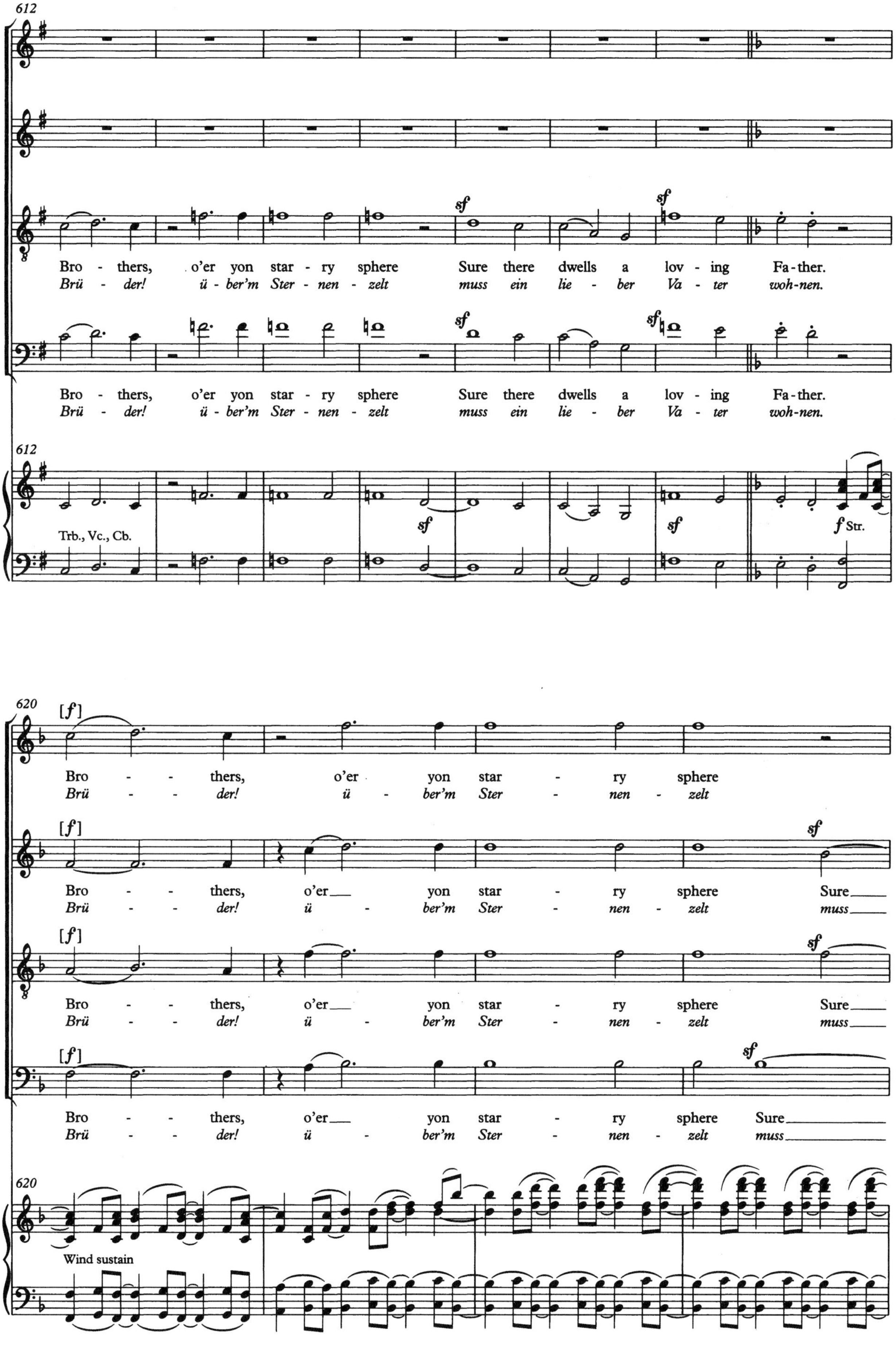
612
sf
sf
Bro - thers, o'er yon star - ry sphere Sure there dwells a lov - ing Fa-ther.
Brü - der! ü - ber'm Ster - nen - zelt muss ein lie - ber Va - ter woh-nen.
sf
sf
Bro - thers, o'er yon star - ry sphere Sure there dwells a lov - ing Fa-ther.
Brü - der! ü - ber'm Ster - nen - zelt muss ein lie - ber Va - ter woh-nen.
612
Trb., Vc., Cb.
sf
sf
f Str.
620
[f]
Bro - - thers, o'er yon star - ry sphere
Brü - - der! ü - ber'm Ster - nen - zelt
[f]
sf
Bro - - thers, o'er yon star - ry sphere Sure
Brü - - der! ü - ber'm Ster - nen - zelt muss
[f]
sf
Bro - - thers, o'er yon star - ry sphere Sure
Brü - - der! ü - ber'm Ster - nen - zelt muss
[f]
sf
Bro - - thers, o'er yon star - ry sphere Sure
Brü - - der! ü - ber'm Ster - nen - zelt muss
620
Wind sustain

624
sf
Sure there dwells a lov - ing Fa - ther.
muss ein lie - ber Va - ter woh - nen.
there dwells a lov - ing Fa - ther.
ein lie - ber Va - ter woh - nen.
there dwells a lov - ing Fa - ther.
ein lie - ber Va - ter woh - nen.
there dwells a lov - ing Fa - ther.
ein lie - ber Va - ter woh - nen.
Fl., Cl., Bsn.
Vc.
p
628
Adagio ma non troppo ma divoto (𝅗𝅥 = 60)
p
cresc.
O ye mil-lions kneel be -
Ihr stürzt nie - der, Mil - li -
cresc.
p

635
pp cresc.
ff
pp
cresc.
- fore Him, World, dost feel thy Ma - ker near? Seek Him o'er yon star - ry
- o - nen? Ah - nest du den Schöp-fer, Welt? Such' ihn ü - ber'm Ster - nen -
- fore Him, World, dost feel thy Ma - ker near? Seek Him o'er yon star - ry
- o - nen? Ah - nest du den Schöp-fer, Welt? Such' ihn ü - ber'm Ster - nen -
- fore Him, World, dost feel___ thy Ma - ker near? Seek Him o'er yon star - ry
- o - nen? Ah - nest du___ den Schöp-fer, Welt? Such' ihn ü - ber'm Ster - nen -
- fore Him, World, dost feel thy Ma - ker near? Seek Him o'er yon star - ry
- o - nen? Ah - nest du den Schöp-fer, Welt? Such' ihn ü - ber'm Ster - nen -
635
pp
cresc.
ff
p
pp
cresc.
643
f
ff
sf
sphere, O'er the stars en - thron'd, a - dore Him!
- zelt! Ü - ber Ster - nen muss er woh - nen,
sphere, O'er___ the stars en - thron'd, a - dore Him!
- zelt! Ü - ber Ster - nen muss er woh - nen,
sphere, O'er the stars en - thron'd, a - dore Him!
- zelt! Ü - ber Ster - nen muss er woh - nen,
sphere, O'er the stars en - thron'd, a - dore Him!
- zelt! Ü - ber Ster - nen muss er woh - nen,
643
8
f
ff
pp Str.

651
pp
O'er the stars en -
über Sternen
O'er the
über
Wind
sempre pp
Timp.
653
- thron'd, a - dore Him!
muss er wohnen.
stars en - thron'd, a - dore Him!
Sternen muss er wohnen.

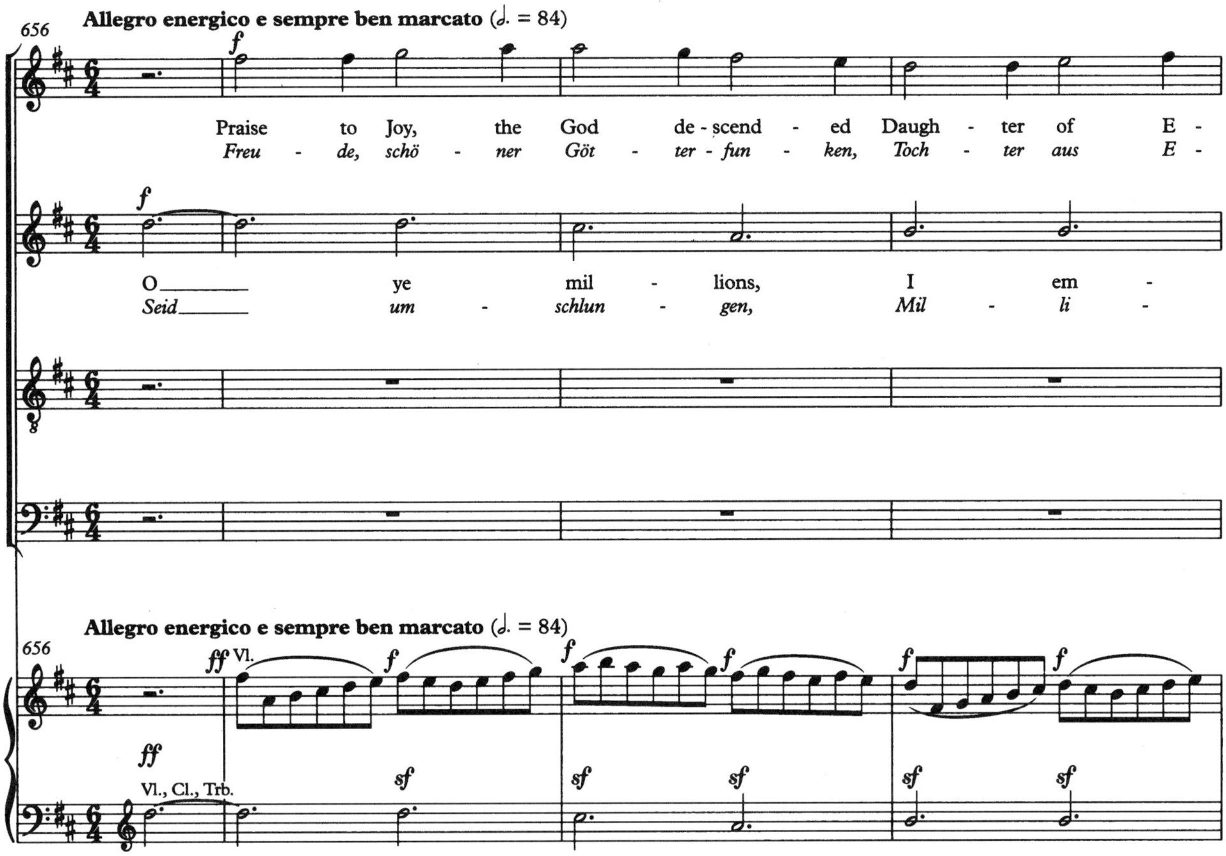

656

Allegro energico e sempre ben marcato (𝅗𝅥. = 84)

Praise to Joy, the God descended Daughter of E-
Freude, schöner Götterfunken, Tochter aus E-

O ye millions, I em-
Seid umschlungen, Milli-

Allegro energico e sempre ben marcato (𝅗𝅥. = 84)

656

ff Vl. f f f f f

ff Vl., Cl., Trb. sf sf sf sf sf

660

-lysium, Ray of mirth and rapture blended, Goddess, to thy
-lysium, wir betreten feuertrunken, Himmlische, dein

-brace ye! Here's a joyful kiss for
-onen! Diesen Kuss der ganzen

660

f f f f f f f f

664
shrine we come. Praise her!
Hei - lig - tum! Freu - de!
[f]
all! O ye mil - lions, I em -
Welt! Seid um - schlun - gen, Mil - li -
f
O ye mil - lions, I em -
Seid um - schlun - gen, Mil - li -
[f]
Praise to Joy, the God de-scend - ed Daugh - ter of E -
Freu - de, schö - ner Göt - ter - fun - ken, Toch - ter aus E -
664
f
ff Wind sustain
Bsn., Contrabsn., Vc., Cb.
668
Praise her! Hail, O God - dess, to thy shrine
Freu - de! Wir be - tre - ten dein Hei - -
- brace ye! Here's a joy - ful kiss for
- o - nen! Die - sen Kuss der gan - zen
- brace ye! Here's a joy - ful kiss for
- o - nen! Die - sen Kuss der gan - zen
- ly - si - um, Ray of mirth and rap - ture blend - ed, God - dess, to thy
- ly - si - um, wir be - tre - ten feu - er - trun - ken, Himm - li - sche, dein
668
sf
sf

672
all!
Welt!
Praise her!
Freu - de!
all! Praise to Joy, the God de-scend - ed Daugh - ter of E -
Welt! Freu - de, schö - ner Göt - ter-fun - ken, Toch - ter aus E -
ff
shrine we come. O ye mil - lions, I em -
Hei - lig-tum! Seid um - schlun - gen, Mil - li -
672
ff
f
676
we come.
lig - tum!
Praise her! Hail, O God - dess to thy shrine we
Freu - de! Wir be - tre - ten dein Hei - lig -
-ly - si - um, Ray of mirth and rap - ture blend - ed, God - dess, to thy
-ly - si - um, Wir be - tre - ten feu - er-trun - ken, Himm - li-sche, dein
-brace ye! Here's a joy - ful kiss for
-o - nen! Die - sen Kuss der gan - zen
676
f

680
O ye mil - lions, I em -
Seid um - schlun - gen, Mil - li -
come. Praise to Joy, the God de-scend - ed Daugh - ter of E -
- tum! Freu - de, schö - ner Göt - ter - fun - ken, Toch - ter aus E -
shrine we come. Praise her!
Hei - lig - tum! Freu - de!
all,
Welt,
680
ff
684
- brace ye! Here's a joy - ful kiss for
- o - nen! Die - sen Kuss der gan - zen
- ly - si - um, Ray of mirth and rap - ture blend - ed, God - dess, to thy
- ly - si - um, Wir be - tre - ten feu - er - trun - ken, Himm - li - sche, dein
Praise her! Hail, O God - dess, to thy shrine
Freu - de! Wir be - tre - ten dein Hei - -
Here's a
die - sen
684

688
all, Here's a joy - ful kiss for
Welt, die - sen Kuss der gan - zen
shrine we come. Hail, God - - -
Hei - lig - tum, dein Hei - - -
we come, to thy
- - - - lig - tum, dein
joy - ful kiss for all, Here's a
Kuss der gan - zen Welt, die - sen
688
f f f f f f f
692
all, a kiss for all! Praise to Joy, the
Welt, der gan - zen Welt! Freu - de, schö - ner
ff
- dess, hail! O ye
- lig - tum! Seid um -
shrine
Hei - - - - - - -
joy - ful kiss for all!
Kuss der gan - zen Welt!
692
f f f f f

696
God de-scend - ed Daugh - ter of E - ly - si - um, O God - dess, to thy
Göt - ter - fun - ken, wir be - tre - ten feu - er - trun - ken, Himm - li - sche, dein
mil - lions, I em - brace ye! Here's a
- schlun - gen, Mil - li - o - nen! Die - sen
we
lig -
Praise her! Praise her! Hail, O
Freu - de! Freu - de! wir be -
696
700
shrine we come, O ye
Hei - lig - tum! Seid um -
sf sf sf
joy - ful kiss for all! Praise to Joy, the
Kuss der gan - zen Welt! Freu - de, schö - ner
come, to thee we come! O ye
- tum, dein Hei - lig - tum! Seid um -
God - dess, to thy shrine we come!
- tre - ten dein Hei - lig - tum!
700
f f

704
mil - lions,
O
ye
-schlun - gen,
seid
um -
God de-scend - ed Daugh - ter of E - ly - si - um,
Ray of mirth and
Göt - ter-fun - ken, Toch - ter aus E - ly - si - um,
wir be - tre - ten
mil - lions, I em - brace
-schlun - gen, seid um - schlun - - - - -
O
ye mil - lions, Here's a
Seid
um - schlun - gen! Die - sen
704
f
ff
f
f
f
708
mil - lions, I em - brace ye, I em -
-schlun - gen, Mil - li - o - nen, Mil - - - li -
rap - ture blend - ed, God - dess to thy shrine we come. O ye
feu - er-trun - ken, Himm - li-sche, dein Hei - lig-tum! Seid um -
ye,
O
ye
- - - - gen,
seid
um -
joy - ful kiss for all! Praise to Joy, the
Kuss der gan - zen Welt! Freu - de, schö - ner
708

712
- brace ye, Here's a kiss, here's a
- o - nen! Die - sen Kuss, die - - sen
mil - lions, I em - brace ye, Here's a
- schlun - gen, Mil - li - o - nen! Die - sen
mil - lions, I em - brace ye, Here's a
- schlun - gen, Mil - li - o - nen! Die - sen
God de-scend - ed Daugh - ter of E - ly - si - um, Ray of mirth and
Göt - ter-fun - ken, Toch - ter aus E - ly - si - um, wir be - tre - ten
712
716
joy - ful kiss for all, a kiss for
Kuss der gan - zen Welt, der gan - zen
joy - ful, joy - ful kiss for all!
Kuss der gan - zen, gan - zen Welt!
joy - ful kiss for all!
Kuss der gan - zen Welt!
rap - ture blend - ed, God - dess, to thy shrine we come.
feu - er-trun - ken, Himm - li - sche, dein Hei - - lig - tum!
716

720
ff
all,
Welt,
[ff]
Praise to Joy, the God de - scend - ed
Freu - de, schö - ner Göt - ter - fun - ken,
sf sf sf ff
a kiss for all! O
der gan - zen Welt! Seid
ff
O ye mil - lions,
Seid um - schlun - gen,
720
ff non legato
724
Daugh - ter of E - ly - si - um, God - dess, to thy shrine, to thy
Toch - ter aus E - ly - si - um, wir be - tre - ten, Himm - li - sche, dein
ye mil - lions, I em - brace ye,
um - schlun - gen, Mil - li - o - nen!
I em - brace ye, Here's a joy - ful
Mil - li - o - nen! Die - sen Kuss der
724

728
— a kiss for all!
— der gan - zen Welt!
shrine we come!
Hei - - - - - - lig - tum!
Here's a joy - ful kiss for all!
Die - - sen Kuss der gan - zen Welt!
joy - ful kiss for all!
gan - zen, gan - - - - zen Welt!
728
732
World, dost feel thy
Ah - nest du den
O ye mil - lions, kneel be - fore Him.
Ihr stürzt nie - der, Mil - li - o - nen,
732
Cl., Bsn.
pp Str.

738
[p] cresc.
Seek Him o'er yon star - ry sphere,
Such' ihn ü - ber'm Ster - nen - zelt,
Ma - ker near?
Schö - pfer, Welt?
738
Ob.
cresc.
744
cresc.
Seek Him o'er yon star - ry sphere, Bro - thers! Bro - thers!
such' ihn ü - ber'm Ster - nen - zelt. Brü - der! Brü - der!
744
Fl.
Str.
Wind

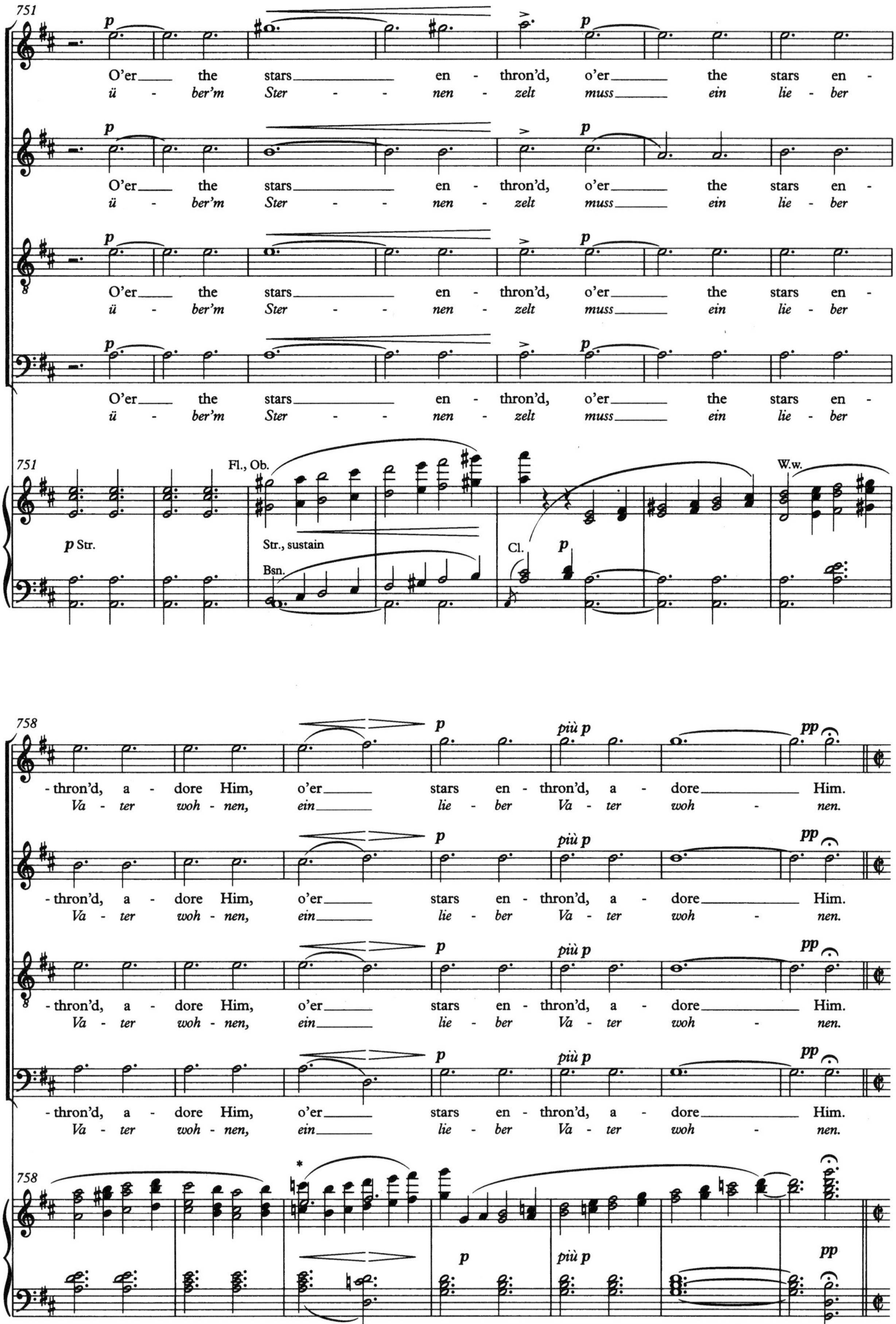
751
p
O'er the stars en - thron'd, o'er the stars en -
ü - ber'm Ster - - nen - zelt muss ein lie - ber
p
O'er the stars en - thron'd, o'er the stars en -
ü - ber'm Ster - - nen - zelt muss ein lie - ber
p
O'er the stars en - thron'd, o'er the stars en -
ü - ber'm Ster - - nen - zelt muss ein lie - ber
p
O'er the stars en - thron'd, o'er the stars en -
ü - ber'm Ster - - nen - zelt muss ein lie - ber
751
p Str.
Fl., Ob.
Str., sustain
Bsn.
Cl.
p
W.w.
758
p
più p
pp
- thron'd, a - dore Him, o'er stars en - thron'd, a - dore Him.
Va - ter woh - nen, ein lie - ber Va - ter woh - nen.
- thron'd, a - dore Him, o'er stars en - thron'd, a - dore Him.
Va - ter woh - nen, ein lie - ber Va - ter woh - nen.
- thron'd, a - dore Him, o'er stars en - thron'd, a - dore Him.
Va - ter woh - nen, ein lie - ber Va - ter woh - nen.
- thron'd, a - dore Him, o'er stars en - thron'd, a - dore Him.
Va - ter woh - nen, ein lie - ber Va - ter woh - nen.
758
*
p
più p
pp

* See Preface

765
Allegro ma non tanto (𝅗𝅥 = 120)
TENOR SOLO
Joy thou
Toch - ter,
BASS SOLO
Joy thou
Toch - ter,
765
Allegro ma non tanto (𝅗𝅥 = 120)
pp
Vln., Vln.
pp
Wind
Vc., Cb.
sempre pp
Bsn.
Vla.
770
SOPRANO SOLO
Joy thou daugh - ter of E - ly - si-um,
Toch - ter, Toch - ter aus E - ly - si-um,
ALTO SOLO
Joy thou daugh - ter of E - ly - si-um,
Toch - ter, Toch - ter aus E - ly - si-um,
daugh-ter of E - ly - si-um,
Toch - ter aus E - ly - si-um,
daugh-ter of E - ly - si-um,
Toch - ter aus E - ly - si-um,
770
Cl.
Ob.

775
Joy thou
Toch - ter,
Joy thou
Toch - ter,
775
Wind
Str.
780
daugh - ter of E - ly - si-um,
Toch - ter aus E - ly - si-um,
By
Dei -
daugh - ter of E - ly - si-um,
Toch - ter aus E - ly - si-um,
Joy thou daugh - ter of E - ly - si-um,
Toch - ter, Toch - ter aus E - ly - si-um,
Joy thou daugh - ter of E - ly - si-um,
Toch - ter, Toch - ter aus E - ly - si-um,
780
Ob.
Cl.
Ob.
Fl.

785
cresc.
— thy ma - gic, by thy ma - gic is — u - ni - ted, — by — thy —
- ne Zau - ber, dei - ne Zau - ber bin - den — wie - der, — dei - ne —
By thy ma - gic, by thy ma - gic is — u - ni - ted,
Dei - ne Zau - ber, dei - ne Zau - ber bin - den — wie - der,
cresc.
By thy ma - gic, by thy ma - gic is — u - ni - ted, —
Dei - ne Zau - ber, dei - ne Zau - ber bin - den — wie - der, —
cresc.
By thy ma - gic,
Dei - ne Zau - ber,
785
pp Wind
Str. pizz.
cresc. poco a poco
790
ma - gic — is — u - ni - ted, — What stern Cus - tom part - ed wide, by —
Zau - ber — bin - den — wie - der — was die Mo - de streng ge - teilt, dei -
cresc.
by thy ma - gic, by thy ma - gic is — u - ni - ted, — yea
dei - ne Zau - ber, dei - ne Zau - ber bin - den — wie - der, — bin - -
ev - - - - er is u - ni - ted, by thy ma - gic,
bin - - - - den, bin - den wie - der, dei - ne Zau - ber,
by thy ma - gic is — u - ni - ted, — by — thy — ma - gic —
dei - ne Zau - ber bin - den — wie - der, — dei - ne — Zau - ber —
790

795
— thy ma - gic, by thy ma - gic, is u - ni - ted
- ne Zau - ber, dei - ne Zau - ber bin - den wie - der,
— by thee u - ni - ted, What
- den, bin - den wie - der, was
by thy ma - gic is u - ni - ted, What stern Cus - tom
dei - ne Zau - ber bin - den wie - der, was die Mo - de
is u - ni - ted, What stern Cus - tom part - -
bin - den wie - der, was die Mo - de streng
Chorus
SOPRANO
p cresc.
By thy ma - gic, by thy ma - gic
Dei - ne Zau - ber, dei - ne Zau - ber
ALTO
TENOR
BASS
cresc.
Str. arco

799
What stern Cus-tom part - - - - - ed wide.
was die Mo - de streng ge - teilt.
— stern Cus-tom part - - - - - ed wide.
— die Mo - de streng ge - teilt.
part - - - - - - - ed wide.
streng ge - teilt.
- - - - - - - ed wide.
ge - teilt.
799
is u - ni - ted, is u - ni - ted What stern Cus - tom
bin - den wie - der, bin - den wie - der, was die Mo - de
is u - ni - ted, is u - ni - ted What stern Cus - tom
bin - den wie - der, bin - den wie - der, was die Mo - de
is u - ni - ted, is u - ni - ted What stern Cus - tom
bin - den wie - der, bin - den wie - der, was die Mo - de
is u - ni - ted, is u - ni - ted What stern Cus - tom
bin - den wie - der, bin - den wie - der, was die Mo - de
799
Tutti

804
(Chorus)
part - - - ed wide.
streng ge - teilt.
All man-
Al - le
ff
p cresc.
8
809
- kind are bro - thers plight - ed, all man-kind, yea, all man - kind are bro - thers
Men - schen, al - le Men - schen, al - le Men - schen, al - le Men-schen wer - den
Poco adagio
Poco Adagio
cresc.
sf
Vln.
p express.
Wind

813

Tempo I

plight-ed, Where thy gen - tle wings a - bide.
Brü - der, wo dein sanf - ter Flü - gel weilt.

plight-ed, Where thy gen - tle wings a - bide.
Brü - der, wo dein sanf - ter Flü - gel weilt.

plight-ed, Where thy gen - tle wings a - bide.
Brü - der, wo dein sanf - ter Flü - gel weilt.

plight - ed, Where thy gen - tle wings a - bide.
Brü - der, wo dein sanf - ter Flü - gel weilt.

813

p dolce

Tempo I

Wind

818

p cresc.

By thy ma-gic, by thy ma-gic is u - ni - ted
Dei - ne Zau-ber, dei - ne Zau-ber bin - den wie - der,

By thy ma-gic, by thy ma-gic is u - ni - ted
Dei - ne Zau-ber, dei - ne Zau-ber bin - den wie - der,

By thy ma-gic, by thy ma-gic is u - ni - ted
Dei - ne Zau-ber, dei - ne Zau-ber bin - den wie - der,

By thy ma-gic, by thy ma-gic is u - ni - ted
Dei - ne Zau-ber, dei - ne Zau-ber bin - den wie - der,

818

cresc.

824
What stern Cus - tom part - - - ed wide.
was die Mo - de streng ge - teilt.
Tutti
p cresc.
829
SOPRANO SOLO
ALTO SOLO
TENOR SOLO
BASS SOLO
All man - kind are bro - thers
Al - le Men-schen, al - le,
Chorus
All man-kind, yea, all man-kind are bro - thers plight - ed, bro - thers
Al - le Men-schen, al - le Men-schen, al - le Men-schen, al - le

834
Poco Adagio
div.
cresc.
unis.
plight - ed, all are bro - thers plight - ed, Where thy gen - - - -
al - le Men - schen wer - den Brü - der, wo dein sanf - - - -
plight - ed, all are bro - thers plight - ed, Where thy gen - - - -
al - le Men - schen wer - den Brü - der, wo dein sanf - - - -
plight - ed, all are bro - thers plight - ed, Where thy gen - - - -
al - le Men - schen wer - den Brü - der, wo dein sanf - - - -
plight - ed, all are bro - thers plight - ed, Where thy gen - - - -
al - le Men - schen wer - den Brü - der, wo dein sanf - - - -
834
Poco Adagio
plight - ed.
Men-schen.
plight - ed.
Men-schen.
plight - ed.
Men-schen.
plight - ed.
Men-schen.
834
Poco Adagio
Cl., Bsn.
Str.

838
- - - - - tle wings a - bide,
- - - - - ter Flü - gel weilt,
- - - - - tle_ wings a - bide,
- - - - - ter_ Flü - gel weilt,
- - - - - - - - tle_
- - - - - - - - ter_
- - tle wings a - bide, thy
- - ter Flü - gel weilt, dein
838
841
cresc.
thy gen - - - - tle wings a - bide.
dein sanf - - - - ter Flü - gel_ weilt.
cresc.
thy gen - - - - tle wings a - bide.
dein sanf - - - - ter Flü - gel_ weilt.
cresc.
wings a - bide, thy gen - tle wings a - bide.
Flü - gel weilt, dein sanf - ter Flü - gel_ weilt.
cresc.
gen - - - - - tle wings a - bide.
sanf - - - - - ter Flü - gel weilt.
841

* Probably **Presto**, see Preface

860
kiss for all, a kiss for all!
gan-zen Welt, der gan-zen Welt!
kiss for all, a kiss for all!
gan-zen Welt, der gan-zen Welt!
kiss for all, a kiss for all!
gan-zen Welt, der gan-zen Welt!
kiss for all, a kiss for all!
gan-zen Welt, der gan-zen Welt!
8
860
sf
sf
f
f
866
Bro-thers, o'er yon star-ry sphere, o'er yon star-ry
Brü-der, ü-berm Ster-nen-zelt muss ein lie-ber
Bro-thers, o'er yon star-ry sphere, o'er yon star-ry
Brü-der, ü-berm Ster-nen-zelt muss ein lie-ber
Bro-thers, o'er yon star-ry sphere, o'er yon star-ry
Brü-der, ü-berm Ster-nen-zelt muss ein lie-ber
Bro-thers, o'er yon star-ry sphere, o'er yon star-ry
Brü-der, ü-berm Ster-nen-zelt muss ein lie-ber
8
866
f
f
f
f
f

871
sphere, Sure there dwells a lov - ing Fa - - - - ther, there
Va - ter, ein lie - ber Va - ter woh - - - - nen, ein
871
876
dwells a lov - ing Fa-ther. O ye mil-lions, I em-brace ye!
lie - ber Va - ter woh-nen. Seid um-schlun-gen, seid um-schlun-gen!
876

882
ff
Here's a joy - ful kiss for all, a kiss for all, a
Die - sen Kuss der gan - zen Welt, der gan - zen Welt, der
888
sf
kiss for all, here's a joy - ful kiss for all, a
gan - zen Welt, die - sen Kuss der gan - zen Welt, der
f

894
ff
ff
kiss for all, a joy - ful, joy
gan - zen Welt, der gan - zen, gan
kiss for all, a joy - ful,___ joy
gan - zen Welt, der gan - zen,___ gan
f
f
ff
f
8
900
- ful kiss, a kiss for all!
- zen Welt, der gan zen Welt!
- ful___ kiss, a kiss for all!
- zen___ Welt, der gan zen Welt!

906
Praise her!
Freu - de.
Praise to Joy, the God de - scend-ed,
Freu - de, schö - ner Göt - ter - fun - ken,
Joy, the
schö - ner
f
ff
912
God de - scend-ed,
Göt - - - ter - fun - ken,
Daugh -
Töch -
ff

918
Maestoso (♩ = 60)
ter of E - ly - si-um,
ter aus E - ly - si-um,
Joy, O Joy, the
Freu - de schö - - ner
Vl. & Fl.
cresc.
Str.
Wind sustain
921
God de-scend - ed, God de - scend - ed.
Göt - ter-fun - ken, Göt - ter - fun - ken.
Prestissimo *
Tutti sempre ff

* See Preface

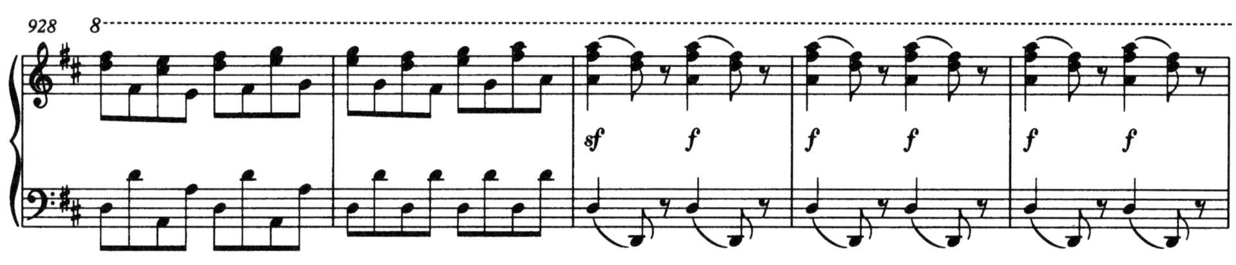

Music origination by
Barnes Music Engraving Ltd, East Sussex.